T0145183

Maggie

The Life of a Little Girl in Ghana, Africa

Amy Brummit

AuthorHouse™
1663 Liberty Drive
Bloomington, IN 47403
www.authorhouse.com
Phone: 1 (800) 839-8640

© 2015 Amy Brummit. All rights reserved.

A percentage of proceeds from the sale of this book will go to help fund Maggie's education.

No part of this book may be reproduced, stored in a retrieval system,
or transmitted by any means without the written permission of the author.

Published by AuthorHouse: 8/26/2015

ISBN: 978-1-5049-3375-9 (sc)
978-1-5049-3376-6 (e)

Print information available on the last page.

Any people depicted in stock imagery provided by Thinkstock are models,
and such images are being used for illustrative purposes only.
Certain stock imagery © Thinkstock.

This book is printed on acid-free paper.

Because of the dynamic nature of the Internet, any web addresses or links contained in this book may have changed
since publication and may no longer be valid. The views expressed in this work are solely those of the author and do
not necessarily reflect the views of the publisher, and the publisher hereby disclaims any responsibility for them.

Dedication

For Maggie, who helped me to understand - AJB

For the estimated two million people in Paraguay
who lack access to clean water - CCNH

In Ghana, Africa, a little girl named Maggie lives in the village of Nkwantekese. Maggie is a special little girl who always has a smile on her face.

She lives with her aunt because her mom and dad cannot take care of her.

Yes, and Maggie smiles.

Maggie walks to a pond three times a day to get water. She must carry the heavy bucket of water back to her home for cooking and cleaning.

Yes, and Maggie smiles.

Maggie helps her aunt pound fufu which is the main meal of the day. It comes from the cassava plant and they will have to pound it for several hours before they can eat it.

Yes, and Maggie smiles.

Maggie helps her aunt do the laundry for the rest of the family.

Yes, and Maggie smiles.

Maggie takes a bucket bath when washing because her home does not have running water.

Yes, and Maggie smiles.

Maggie goes to the market with her aunt to buy food and to visit friends from the other villages.

Yes, and Maggie smiles.

Maggie has one doll she loves playing with. This is Maggie's only toy.

Yes, and Maggie smiles.

Maggie cannot always go to school because her family does not have the money to pay for school.

Yes, and Maggie smiles.

Maggie is shy so she watches the other children in the village as they play together.

18

Yes, and Maggie smiles.

Maggie likes to watch the other kids in the village play soccer.

Yes, and Maggie smiles.

21

Maggie uses a stick to draw pictures in the dirt because she does not have crayons, pencils or paper.

Yes, and Maggie smiles.

Maggie often watches the people in her village dancing and drumming.

24

Yes, and Maggie smiles.

When Maggie is sick, she cannot go to a doctor because the doctor is too far away and costs too much money.

Yes, and Maggie smiles.

Maggie goes to church with her aunt every Sunday.

Yes, and Maggie smiles.

Maggie watches the beautiful sun set over Ghana.

Yes, and Maggie smiles.

Amy Brummit was an elementary teacher for many years in far-flung places such as Ghana, China and Paraguay.

She loves the magic of children's books and knows first hand how children light up and learn from them.

Originally from Bloomington, Indiana, USA, she is currently living and working in Antarctica to support scientific research.

Camila Cáceres Neri Huerta was born in Paraguay, South America in 1993.

She loves working with children as a first grade instructional assistant at the American School of Asuncion.

She is also currently studying psychology at the Catholic University Nuestra Señora de la Asunción and lives with her family in Paraguay.

Printed in the United States
By Bookmasters